TAXI NIGHT

TAXI NIGHT

Cliff Fyman

★

LONG NEWS BOOKS, 2021
Brooklyn

PART 1

TAXI NIGHT

I WANT YOU TO STOP!
Like, don't go with me!
I'm sure it's fine.
Maybe I don't
need to go, I don't
know, maybe I should
just wait till morning.
Like, I don't know!
If I wait another hour
or two you're just going
to get mad at me even more
for not going to the hospital
sooner.
I don't want to waste
money it's like you're *so*
annoyed this is exactly what
I mean—look at you!
LOOK AT YOU!
No! Look at how you treated me
since I told you I wanted
to go to the hospital.
What are you talking about?
What are you talking about?
What was all of that?
What was all of that stupid shit
on the couch?
Guess what, Joe.
That i.v. helped me, that i.v.
they gave me got rid of it.
You know what?
You're not them.
I'm not going to just sit there
if I have a blood clot
so just shut the fuck up!

No, it's like you want me
to sit there in pain.
Stop!
If they don't believe me
I'll never go to that hospital again.
I'm not lying.
Do you think
I need to be dealing with this?
No!
It's like every single time
that I'm sick
you make it worse!
Yeah you do.
We're going to get divorced over this.
Ok?
What was that on the couch?
What was that about?
How you're trying to tell me
what to tell them.
I don't need you yelling at me.
It makes me look bad.
All your little eye rolls
and all your little whatever.
What I need to deal with
is my husband on top of all this?
Like it's not bad enough? Like I'm not
worried enough?

★

They're twin brothers
late 30s
and they live together
and they came out to their
family and their family

4

is, like, ok but why don't
you each live separately
and meet someone and settle
down and have kids and
they're, like, we don't want to
meet anyone we like each
other and the family is, like,
ok and the brothers are
quiet about it because
there could be laws
against
it.

★

                    I
made the biggest meal for
everyone on *Rosh Hashanah*.
Do you remember? Every
Jewish holiday is getting
so expensive it's ridiculous.
I'm not making a meal
after *Yom Kippur*.
Craig is Italian.
The mother's boyfriend is
Protestant. Ashley's kids
have dropped out of Talmud
Torah. What fast are
they breaking? No one's
fasting.

★

Boo-Boo, you're my baby.
Once a week, once every two weeks.
I got my business. I respect your business, babe.
Heh-heh. We're going to create a party, baby
—driver, when you get to 117th bust a left—
we're going to create something *gookey*.
Hold on one second—hel-lo, I'll be there in two minutes,
I'm in a cab already—back to you, Boo-Boo! You can come by,
let me see how go-o-o-d you're lookin'.
So when we going to make this date?
I need to poke you, Boo-Boo. When
can I see you? Stop all this foolishness now.
When? Tomorrow? Thursday? Talk to me. I understand
what you're doing. You got a friend. You got to
do what you got to do. You got to be easy
—first building on the corner—
I don't want to have to bash his head in.
He'll think 'let me get the license plate
of that truck'—heh heh heh!
What happened? What happened?
I don't understand. We were like this!
You've been banned, fella. Heh-heh-heh.
—right here's good, driver—

★

My sister she, like, had
this operation down there,
you know, to 'rejuvenate,'
because she thought
she wasn't pretty enough
to get remarried so she saved up
paid for the surgery
didn't tell my parents.
The doctor did an okay

6

job. Then she married
a loser anyway and had
another kid.
        Your sister married a
        person who sucks?
        That sucks.
And when she had the surgery
I took care
of her because she was
sore, and I took care
of her daughter too.

★

She's, like, VERY pregnant
and comes bopping up
in a jumper WITHOUT
a shirt and from the side
all you can see is, like,
BRA. Some people fit
into our culture and some don't.
She comes to work looking
VERY Sunday morning.

★

Listen, you want to fight
me? I'm gonna punch
your shit and send you
back to prison so suck
my prison dick. You know
you like to suck this dick,
bitch. You know you always

7

think about his dick.

  'We were together
at around age 11. I never
think
about his dick
a day in my life.'

  You want
that really bad bad dick.

  And you, driver.
  Thanks
for telling me what
to do.
Now you get no tip.

Slam!

  ★

Yo, yo. Astoria Boulevard, make a right, take the highway,
and you a good brother.
Thank you so much
FOR PICKIN' ME UP.
It's sad.
I'm a good black guy
and I can't get a fucking taxi!
Damn!
That's bullshit.
Where you from?
  I'm from here.
  I grew up with white and black.
No, where you from? You white? Where? Where?
Are you white or Spanish? Puerto Rican?

(Silence)
I'm Jewish.
JEWISH?! AND YOU DRIVING A TAXI?
O my gosh! I work for Jewish people,
and I don't want to hear anything.
These mothers have money.
Look, brother, you good, man. Exactly.
Oh, you are so good.
Go onto that highway, Grand Central,
you are good.
Damn, you a Jewish guy.
Fuck you doing driving cars?
Really? Seriously? Nah, man, I don't
believe that. You ain't Jewish.
Jewish people I work for
they got millions and millions
of dollars. They so cheap.
Even if I had a recorder,
if I was on ABC I'd say this shit too.
Cheap, man.
They got so much money.

I had a good time tonight.
I'm a bartender.
You know how much money I spent tonight?
I made $220, I spent $140,
and I'm about to go spend some more money.
I got to pay this fare, right?

★

Come closer. You've done
enough. I did my
numbers today.
20 million this year and 21

million next year. If I had
20 people to each buy a
million but I don't.
The thing about moving all this
money is that it doesn't
create anything. It's just
making money by moving it
from one place to another.

★

Dad, my son said he's been
a Met fan his whole life
and doesn't want his baby boy
to have to go through that.
Is it all right
if he makes him a Yankee fan?

★

One summer Sunday afternoon Washington Heights a 29 year-old woman said at age 18 she was a man who had a sex change. She took my taxi instead of the subway to avoid being stared at. As a gay teen she couldn't relate to the scene. Besides, her mother was a strict Baptist opposed to same-sex activity. She figured if she became a woman then slept with a guy she'd be okay in the eyes of the Bible. When she first inquired about hormone treat-ment she said a doctor rushed her into the sex change which she now regretted.

★

You can't imagine how
hard it is to raise two
kids under two years old.
Men don't get it. Ordering
diapers. Ordering shoes.
A check list. I could
jump out the window!

★

Having short hair is just
a weird psychology
trip. Do I like it? It's
just that guys treat me
differently with short hair.
This girl I was
living with said she wanted
to cut off all her hair so I
said if you do it I'll do it.
I hate writing fiction I love
writing poetry. I'm, like,
whatever. I like eyes.
I'll fuck a guy
because of his eyes.
That might be weird
but that's how I am.
Like, Drug Doug.
I can't fuck with his
roommate but his
roommate can fuck with
me. Today. Like,
whatever. I don't know.
Like, Mark's way better.
2nd and 7th, please!
I try to spend as much

money on my credit card
as possible.

★

Let's keep this in perspective.
This is a 75 thousand to
150 thousand dollar book
deal. It's not a million
dollar deal with a ten percent
advance of one hundred
thousand dollars.

★

Driver, do you think this world
is going to survive another 100 years?
Tsunamis, earthquakes, frack oil drilling,
slant oil drilling. We're digging in Texas
but at an angle under the Rio Grande
so we can steal Mexico's oil at a slant.
Slant oil.
Polar ice caps melting, ozones splitting apart.
China's cheating for war, Korea wants war.
46 percent of Africa has AIDS,
and Africa's a continent not a country.
Indians and Pakistanis.
Jews and Arabs.
In Florida they had people voting
who were dead fifty years.
They had foreigners voting twice!
It cannot. It cannot survive
another 100 years. No way.

12

I don't know what to tell my children.
Go to college? Get a good job?
Germ warfare, biological warfare.
Give me change of this.
I'd tip you but it's my last bill.
Have a good fucking day, my man.

I'm not very smart.
I'll be honest. I just strongly
like the sound of sirens.
I'll be honest I'm not very
smart. An ambulance
when it's coming from the
side sounds one way—
whirrrr! Then when it passes
sounds completely
different. Or am I insane?

   Is this my favorite mayor
in the world? This is
       Gaston.
              How are you doing?
I'd like to extend an invitation
       to join us for dinner
this Sunday eve. We'd love
              to host you.

Hello, Eddis.
      This is Gaston.

                    Are you alone?
Can you talk?
             Senators
Simpson and Bowles
          are coming. I think
     we shall set up a buffet.
          Let each gentleman help
                         himself.
We'll go over
what we talked about.

Ok, pal.
See you soon

and remember

if you don't have a seat
at the table
you're probably on the menu.

        ★

Driver, how was your night?
Mine was wack!
I'm a rapper and I'm supposed to
bring people in but no one came.
I feel so low.
I just want to have one more
rum maybe some grass
and go to bed
and call one of my ex's
to come over
and give me a body rub.
Nothing complicated.
I don't want to give of myself.

I just want him to rub me.
Driver, do you think that's ok?

It sounds comforting.

Comforting!
That's the right word.
You sound like a nice guy.
Driver, are you married?
What a catch!
What do you like to do?
This might sound weird
but would you like to rub my legs?
Could you pull over when we get there
and let me sit up front?
We could talk.
The good thing about these jeans
is they have slits in them
so you can reach in
and touch what you like.
Let me show you.

Thank you for taking us, sir. We're homeless.
    Do you have money?
No, sir.
    You don't have any money?
No, sir.
    I'm sorry I can't take you.
Someone could be nice and take us.
    No, I really, it's...
There were about ten cabs going by
some stopped
but none of them would take us.

Come on, sir. We need to go to a hospital.
I could show you the papers.
They gave me this to wear on my wrist.
  Yeah, but I'm not here to do that.
  It's different.
Sir, we're homeless.
  There are places to go for help.
  This is not it. I'm working.
  Besides, you could take a subway.
Will you give us money then for a subway?
  You're taking advantage. No!
Don't get angry. We'll sit here.
You could talk nicely.
  You asked if I'd drive you
  free to 28th & 3rd.
  We're on 77th Street.
  The answer is
  no.
Don't get out. Just sit here.
Let's get out.
No, let's just sit here....

 ★

I'm so happy to be in
Soho. No, no—you
dumped me for this
bitch. You didn't dump
me till you met her
a stripper I might add.
You like a stripper bitch.
Let her suffer. I was a
stripper too but I quit.
Oh, like, hate me.
If you are with another

bitch just tell me you are
with another bitch. It's
not that hard. Oh, well.
It's all good. Now you see
why you and I can't.
You sick warmongering
bitch. Like she texted me—
Today I see you took
the curtains off. I'm
cleaning her out, taking
everything that moves,
everything that crawls.
I'm, like, don't push.
I'm going to have my
husband kill you.

★

Hi!
How are you?
I say how are you?
I'm so late for
yoga I'm taking
a cab.
I've been getting in
a 12-hour work day.
It's brutal!
Some days I do
two-a-days. I love yoga.
It's so great!

★

Hi. My name is Billy.
I have a suit that's ready
to be picked up. I'll come by
on Saturday.
Thank you.

★

I'm heading downtown to the
Gaslight. I don't mean to be
sneaky but price the tickets
at 40 and put out a scare
that there's a shortage
of tickets. I'd like to sell
the place out.

★

Children,
if someone's difficult
and giving you a hard time,
you don't have to...you're not...
it's not like they're assigned to you.
You don't have to get to know them.
But you come from a good mother
so always have underlying love for them.

★

Yo, my n——, I'm coming over
in a cab. Shut the fuck up.

*

Hi, did you say your sprinkler
doesn't work?

*

Mr. Kempner, you said there was
some wood that rotted. Where
is it?

*

He's taking chemo.
Don't tell anyone.
He has some disease.
Makes his organs hard.
When you shake his hand,
it's hard like a prick.

*

I got a DUI last night.
Just out of jail.
Would you take me
to the Bronx?

*

19

Big kiss and I'll call
you from Paris

★

Ostensibly he was mad
at you because why?

★

Everything's good.
Everything's ok.
They're taking out the tubes.

★

A young man coaxed a sobbing young woman
into the back seat and said
from the sidewalk,
as he shut the door,
'I'll call you soon. And remember:
happy birthday.'

★

I'm on my way, baby.

★

Hi, there.
I was wondering.
Could I get
my laundry delivered?

★

I'm the whole reason
this thing is going down,
and you want to chop my
pay? Fuck that!
Fuck that! Fuck that!

★

Hey, Kelly, it's Christopher.
Hey, Gene, it's Christopher.
Tommy, hey, it's Christopher.

★

Sheila, you went dead
on me. Last thing you
said was, 'It was in the
Bronx.'

★

21

A kale salad doesn't sound
like it has any food in it.
Can't we go to a regular
restaurant where I can
order what I want?

★

You know me.
I like being a part of
stuff and not being a part
of stuff.

★

Do you know what Ash
Wednesday is about?
This is the day Jesus went
into the forest for 40 days.
He had some things
to think
about.
Then he was killed.
Ashes
to ashes, dust
to dust.
Here we are. Want to
go to church with me?

★

The priest asked Dan and me
is homosexuality going to get
in the way of your marriage?
What a weird thing to ask.

★

My mother says you
can cry about it or you can
laugh about it so you might
as well laugh about it.

I say you might as well spread
a line on the table and
blow about it.

★

We should run an LPR
on the FDR North 4:20
a.m. perp and see
if we come up with a
black Tahoe. Run a
plate. Any 4 a.m.
action?

★

Seriously, dude, drive safely.

★

All summer he fucking
hit me up and so finally
I slept with him, and now I
tell him you don't want
to hang out with me?
Fuck you! I texted him.
FUCK   YOU!

★

One large pie, one side of
tomato sauce, and one
garlic bread. I think that's
cool. I won't be there
for 20 minutes. Could
you wait a minute
before starting it?

★

Hello. Where you at?

★

Why do you always call
me a dick? That's shit,
man.

*

If you give me a scarf
for Christmas you are
going to get punched
in the dick.
That's a grandma gift.

*

Hi, it's Edith. Could you
text me and let me know
you're still in the land
of the living?

*

Hi, this is Patinski.
Do you still do appraisals?

*

Hi, honey.
Ok.
Well.
Yeah.
Yeah.
I'll weigh it.
Well, honey, honey,
there's nothing I can do

from here.
Don't call me about that.
Honey, honey.
Ok, honey.
I love you.
Bye.

★

They break up and get
back together and then she
claws his face and they break up
and get back together
then he cheats all over the place
they break up
they get back together
then she cheats all over the place
they break up....

★

Buenas noches
Buena note
Buona sera
Bonne nuit
Layla tov
Shukriya
Spako noi nochi
Dobronitz
Bon soir
God natt
Hoda afiz
Oyasumi nasai

Shuboratrei
Wahn ahn
Man ohn
Ratre sawad
Shep behker
Good night.

PART 2

You seem like a neat driver.
Do you mind taking me to Remsen Avenue in Canarsie?
Know how to get there?
How long you been driving cab?
I like the music you got on.
Blues on WKCR?
All right!
Are you married? Got a girlfriend?
A guy like you is alone? I don't believe it!
But I know what it's like.
After a while I felt like, yo, I can't do this forever.
You know what I'm saying?
So that's how you got to feel.
Do you want me to help you find a girl?
(Silence)
I know a lot of women in New York City.
            Ok. I'm listening.
Where do I meet them?
Everywhere!
I go out.
I go to bars.
I go to hookah lounges.
I go to libraries.
I go to art shows.
I even go to poetry contests!
I was up to two girls a day for a while there.
I'm 23, and I'm out all the time, man.
I meet girls everywhere.
What do you have to lose?
We could do a photo shoot of you, right?
Clean you up.
Then what I'll do: I'll match you.
We'll find you ten dates, right?
And then we see what type of women
want to go out with you.
With one you'll do coffee.
With another one you're going to walk

in the um—what's it called?—
in-the-park.
Out of those ten
even if nine are bad
I'm pretty sure you'll be able to find one.
>*You would think so.*
Yessss, man.
And I'm not going to charge you that much.
Of course, I got to make a little money
because I got to get you, like, a nice suit.
>*Yeah—but I'm not—why can't—*
>*I'm not that kind of way. I'm not so formal.*
You got to get formal
if you want to find a good woman!
All right?
Turn right on 4th Avenue.
Left on Atlantic.
So this is how we're going to do it.
I'm going to get you a *good* haircut
and then
off with those grandpa glasses
for the photo shoot.
Put them back on now because you're driving.
All right, king?
I'm going to clean you up.
But first you got to go to boot camp with me.
I got to get you prepared for the date.
You know what I'm saying?
I'm going to bring you back to your old days,
to your ten years ago days, fifteen years ago days,
back when you was a smooth hot shot,
back when you was a top dog player
in the party.
I know you used to go to those parties.
Didn't you, champ?
>*Sure.*
Did you ever do weed?

> *Lots of it.*

Exactly!

You ever did weed with a hot ++ young thing?

> *Sure.*

Exactly!

You want me to bring you back to those days?

Yo, you should take this opportunity.

Be optimistic.

What could go—how could it go—

how could it be any worse at this point?

Let's be honest.

You know what I'm saying?

> *It can't get much worse.*

Exactly!

Maybe a young feller who came in your car

came in your car for a reason

because guess what?

I could probably—I could probably—

turn this into a tv show!

You know what I'm saying?

I can see the t.v. show now: starring Chris Kingsley!

The Young Guy Who Helps the Older Guys Out.

It's usually the other way around

but I'll keep doing it.

And bigger guys with bigger budgets

is gonna help me out!

You know what I'm saying?

More people will hire me!

Yo, man!

Everybody needs somebody

to help him get back in shape.

> *If you have some success with me*
> *the word'll spread.*

Exactly!

Yo, man.

I think we should do this.

At this point, bro, you seem very cool

but I got to be honest with you.
You look like you hit rock bottom
in the love section.
How old are you?
> *Fifty-eight.*

You don't look that.
You know how you look? 40!
> *Thank you.*

You look young, man!
Especially since you shave your beard.
See, imagine you with a haircut
and a nice tailored suit.
You know what I'm saying?
> *You're talkin' wisdom.*

I am talkin' wisdom
because I know what I'm talkin' about!
Check out these photos
on my phone.
This ((bare-breasted)) girl
is the daughter of the
vice-president of Con Edison!
Worse comes to worse
you go on a few dates
with ten great women.
Oh, wow. That's so bad?
A lot of young girls
are into old men right now.
If you want to get them you need *swag*.
Do you still get up?
Yo, I'm going to help you
get your swag back.
You know why you lost your swag?
Because you're driving this cab, man.
Is this job stressing you out?
Don't lie.
Tell me the truth.
I won't judge you.
I promise.

★

My dad and uncle
had a don't-go-to-the-doctor
strategy that
worked for them
but my Mom has a disease
she's dying from
that could've been cured
had she gotten tested sooner.

★

How did she pass away?
She had brain, you know, cancer.
That one Senator Kennedy had.
Glioblastoma multiforme.
I mean, it sounds kind of bad.
Like, I'll really miss her very much.
But.
I think it was better this way.
Would she say it's better this way?
I don't know.
She was in a nursing home.
For the past three months
she was, like, completely paralyzed
except for the little bit of her left arm,
and that was *it*.
She had trouble talking and everything.
So.
At least now she's at peace.
I think.
But.
I saw her three times this week!

So.
I'm glad for that.
But I wasn't really.
Last time I saw her, like,
she was really out of it
then she had this look of, like,
total happiness and joy
when she was looking at me.
So when I looked back I think she kind of knew.
But that I think was a sign
because another friend told me
when his Mom passed away
she suddenly
out of the blue
had this look of total joy.
Then a couple days later
died.
So.
It was kind of weird.
Dying is kind of weird.
I mean. I'm kind of. It sounds terrible.
I'm kind of hap—I mean—
I was very sad.
We made plans for the summer
to do different things and stuff.
But.
I think it's—
for her to live in a nursing home
like that
was not...a good way...to go.
But.
She was really at peace.
She was really happy
when I last saw her
when she woke up.
Yeah.
So.

*Excuse me, do you want the right side
or the left side?*
Oh, on the right hand side, please, driver.
*How do you know she was at peace?
Maybe it was the drugs
that were tranquilizing her.*
No, she wasn't on any medicine
because with brain cancer
you don't have pain, um, because,
like, your nerves are breaking down.
It's actually a very good way to go
because you're not 100 percent
aware of what's happening to you,
if you know what I mean.
Thank you so much
for the ride here, mister.
Bye.

★

Why are you mad at me?
I wanted you to get some food.
And you're arguing because
you want me to go home.
And now it's just changed.
I don't get it.
Stop talking.

That's what I said
get some food
and you said no!
And I was trying
to get you some food
and you said no!

I don't know what to do.
I don't know how
to make you happy
I try and I always fail.

I don't know why
you didn't want to get
a sandwich
I said get a sandwich
and you said no!
I don't get it

I told you I know
I'm pathetic
I told you to get
a sandwich you said no!

What?
I just told you
I'm pathetic
I know I'm pathetic
I know I suck

but I could wait for you
to get a sandwich.

★

A woman would *never*
be arrested standing naked
in an intersection
                    waving a knife!

A woman would *never*
throw a brick

from an overpass
through a car windshield!

A woman would *never*
lure
a seven-year-old boy
                    into a car!

What is wrong with you men?
Clifford, would you tell me
what is wrong with you men?

★

I don't have to smoke pot, baby,
but it makes me eat
and if I don't do that
then I only have one meal a day
and I lose a ton of weight
and I'll become this scrawny little guy
and I don't want to look like that.
You know what I'm saying?
I smoke to fix it out, honey.
Pot is a recreational thing
about to be decriminalized
in every state.
Is that okay? Are you all right with that?
Oh, come on, baby.
When I get the test you want me to get
I will talk to them about my hunger issues.

★

I want a glass of red wine,
oysters and that guy.
What guy? Oh, him, yeah.
We know she can conceive.
She just has to hold it.
The last baby was aborted
after three months because
of a heart defect. She didn't
miscarry. What makes you
like ramen noodles? I had
them in college and miss
them so much! See that
guy my friend James? He's
homeless. He sits in Union
Square park and teaches
people how to play
chess. One night I was wandering
home and, like, watching. Ok.
And he asked me if I'd like to
learn, and I said mmmm. And I
sat down. How much? $20
an hour, and it was *so* good.
I think I'll try for that guy
I met in the elevator. Is he
good looking? He's decent
and handsome and
respectable but not so
good-looking to the point where
you think he's better looking
than you.

★

he witnessed a bar fight at 4 a.m.
a man punched a woman hurt her badly

then the guy ran!
he talked about it
all the way up the fdr
eating two drippy pizza slices
moonlight on the river
his father was born in harlem
he was born in d.c.
and d.c. ain't nothin' like ny
the guy wasn't a man because he ran
how could he hit a woman?

★

I drove a passenger all the way from Wall Street
to South Jamaica then swung around
and parked on a corner
under a crescent moon
and stood on the quiet
Guy Brewer Boulevard sidewalk
where my father used to own a drug store.
For decades he loved that store
until arsonists burned it down—

★

Now there has to be retaliation
until there's no retaliation left.
That's where I'm from, retaliation.
Let's do it.
Let's see who wins.
Let's fucking see.
I've seen him do it with so many people.
But it's different when he does it to me.

You know loyalty and respect
are my first two qualities.
And when you're my best friend
and you break that—I can't—I'm cool.
I'm cool because I'll either have you killed
or I'll deal with you. I'd rather deal with you
than have you killed. You know what I'm saying?

★

If I didn't—multiple sclerosis.
There is something of the
nesting. I could be in Louisiana.
There's a baby due Sept. 15.
I don't even want to wait to
call my parents. This could
give them a heart attack.
I was super-sensitive
to what I told people. I told
Michelle I'm so overwhelmed.
I signed a paper. I haven't
given anyone a dollar.
I'll get the money somehow. Fuck it.
Jean is in Greece
sailing because she's very
stressed out. Here.
You know how many people
Michelle has helped get a baby? Lots.

★

Driver, shake my hand.
I'm going to suck the shit

out of your dick.
I think you need to find
another cab.
No, please, help me find The Living Room!
It's on Metropolitan Avenue.
No one will help me, driver.
No one loves me.
I'll be good.
Please?

★

All the Republicans care about is pro-choice. To stop it.
But when all those babies are born
they want nothing to do with them.

★

The good thing about getting old
is you don't have to worry
about looking young.
No one cares
what you look like
because you're old.
So you can just have fun.

★

I like your skin.
      I like your cock.
Here it is.

I'm just saying.
You can have it.
            Let's wait.
I'm going to fuck the shit out of you
when we get home.
            I hope you will.

★

It's been a complicated
day so I'm just going to sit
here and relax. You have
to think of someone who
will give you strength.
Someone.

★

What are you talking about?
You'll have to step out of the room
            and tell me what you're talking
                        about.
What are you talking about?
What *are* you talking about?

★

Someone walks into your house
and starts to act
like it's his house.
What's the best description?

*

I put my hands on
you no bruises you
can't win the case
and on top of that
on camera you was
making up with me
you lost your case shut up

*

The wake wasn't bad.
Got to see people I hadn't seen in ages.
Just a long day.

*

I only saw them because I went to the bathroom
and they went to the bathroom
and I learned a strange dynamic of their relationship
how at their first meeting
she was wearing a chokehold!
We're, like, weirdos compared to these people.

*

How do you stay married for so long?

★

Are you bisexual yet?

★

I know you're not going to like this
but that's not your baby.

PART 3

I'm so dumb!
Like, why the fuck
am I drinking?
So I woke up today and I'm, like,
I hope I don't get a lot of texts
and he's, like, 'O would you like
to get dinner tonight?'
And I'm, like, I don't know and stuff.
I'll shoot you a draft
after school
because I don't know
what time I'll be free
tomorrow.
And he's, like, 'Ok. So. Are you free
tonight?'
I didn't answer.
He's, like, 'Are you having dinner tonight?'
Question mark.
I didn't answer.
Texts me again
an hour later.
I didn't answer.
So yeah, like,
it was just crazy.
Um, so, like, yeah.
He, like, texts me,
'If this is too much
just let me know I'll stop.'
Dude, I haven't even answered
your first question yet.
And then—
I'm so sorry.
I'm just not looking for anything
new right now.
(I was really
hooking up
hard core

with someone
two months
this summer
but I can't
tell him this.)
He's, like, 'O really?
Because it seems I heard
from other people
last night
you are looking
for something serious.'
I was, like, fuck I was so drunk
I told him I was looking for something
serious
but not with him!
Today I say I'm not looking
for anything serious.
So like OOOPS!
He was, like, 'What happened?'
He came all the way
from Maryland.
He just kept on
texting me, like, non-stop.
And I was, like,
you are fucking annoying.
And I was, like,
what the fuck.

Let's keep on subject
but change it a little bit.
Have you ever had
camel's milk cheese?
Maybe it's just me.

It had some lobster quality to it.
Do you remember?
Some salty lobster thing?
Maybe it's just me.
Shit was weird.
Funky.
Sea-like.
Really weird.
Lewd I would almost call it.

★

I really only like people
who were born after August.

★

Are you going to make
rude mean
comments to me
the rest of my life?

Are you going to tell me
to go to a career center again?
Who do you know with
unlimited resources who
goes to a career center?
Idiots!

★

I'm through with drunken fucking idiots.
I am a drunken fucking idiot!

★

All I know about you
is you make good eggs,
you're an atheist,
and you don't play basketball.
Hello, motherfucker.
Hello, grandpa.
What do you think
of that movie?
I thought it sucked balls.

Here's the thing.
I'm not going to lie to you.
It's, like, the weirdest situation.
We're probably going to break up
once we get back to Greece.

★

Can you imagine?
I've been on my job 27 years.
Can you imagine?
Now they're asking
to see my passport?
If I'm an American citizen.
That kind of deal.
CAN YOU IMAGINE?
I was born in Manhattan
like you.

I don't know
where you were born
but obviously Queens or the Bronx.
I was born in Flower Hospital.
Fifth Avenue.
But fuck.
Really?
27 years
—and now you think
I'm a terrorist threat?

★

I haven't had a good meatball
since my mother passed.

★

I saw you didn't even know who I was.
Yeah you were, Ed. You were!
And what's even more embarrassing
is when somebody who doesn't even really know me,
doesn't know you, asks, like,
"What's wrong with your boyfriend?
Like, are things okay between the two of you?"
You know what? Go to your place tonight.
        Honey.
Yeah, take your stuff, Ed, and go home.
        I was just having fun around the guys.
I saw you didn't even know me.
        I didn't.
Yeah, you did, Ed!
        Honey, I wasn't.

Yeah, you did!
You totally acted that way!
And what's even more embarrassing
is someone who doesn't even know us
is, like, asking me those questions.
You know, it's actually very interesting to me
that you would act that way.
      There we were talking about going to Brazil.
You leaned over like this.
You didn't even lean toward me.
You weren't even.
Your whole body language was odd.
Everything you did was odd.
And you know what?
I didn't say anything to you,
obviously, because we're in a public setting,
we're there together,
when somebody
asks me, you know, like, what's going on between
the two of you?
And what's even worse is everyone there
is fucking married
except for the two of us.
It's, like, you know what?
That's it.
Have a nice life.
You didn't even put your arm around me.
Those are my friends, Ed. Those are my friends
from school.
Those are MY FUCKING FRIENDS.
When my wine was low you didn't notice.
      I wasn't ignoring you.
You were totally ignoring me!
I'm not going to do this anymore.
I'm not going to waste anymore of my time.
I'm not going to get upset over this.
There are a million other guys

who would love to declare to the world
they're with me.
You know what?
I'm going to call some of them up—tonight!
I'm done with this crap.
            That wasn't my intention at all, honey.
That was the body language you were giving off.
            I wasn't giving off any body language.
You know what?
Maybe you just can't handle
an interracial relationship, Ed.
I know now I'm not crazy
for thinking what I've been thinking
and for having these discussions with you
and the discussion
is
over.
Go to my place, pick up your stuff, go home.
I never want to see you again.
Take your boring body language with you.
You're not coming to Brazil.
Fucking embarrassing.

        ✶

            He doesn't have
such a bad life.
Why doesn't he try acupuncture?

    ✶

I don't feel like doing fish
I just want to

55

stick some bird
in the oven
and forget about it.

Paint the apartment.
Shit like that.

*

I just want to pay my
bills. I just want
to pay
my fucking
bills!

*

Hey, cutie, how ya doin'?
You saved me some?
You're rockin' awesome-chawsome!
Can't wait till I get home
to take a bite
out of you!!!

*

I want to come home to you
creating dishes like we did
last night was wonderful
and I want to do that
tonight. I think the decision

is made. I'm one of the
most fortunate people
on the planet.

★

I'll never leave home again
if I ever get home again.

★

That gross asshole finance husband
does coke, strip clubs,
comes home with herpes,
sleeps with her best friends.
Why'd she marry him?

★

You peed in my mouth, sucker!
That's how I know'd
what gender you was.

★

He's very immature when it comes to women
but very mature when it comes to most everything else.

★

We were best friends
ten
minutes. She loosened
my bra.
I said you're so
sweet!
              We went
upstairs. She stopped
talking to me.
People came in.
I was, like,
what?
I don't know.

★

You expect her to be nice.
You bend over backwards
then she treats you
like shit. Why do you keep
trying to get her to be
nice?

★

You don't get it.
I care about the people I care about.
Always.
It doesn't go away because it's over.
Okay? I told you last night

and it's reconfirmed this morning.
I'll never not love you.
What?
I'm not coming to your bed again.
I'm not trying to force anything.
Will you?...in the morning?...ok?...
for me as well...rubbing your feet...
feels like home again.
I was crying because
—you know me.
I know you love me.
Anyway.

Hi, it's me, Daddy.
I hear you're bedridden
with a cold.
I'm so so sorry.
You promise, promise, promise
me you'll take good care of yourself?
I've been working like a dog
all week but it paid off.
I'll call you tomorrow from home
before my opening.
This is your little muffin, Daddy.

What the fuck, motherfucker!

Once you cross that path I will gun for you.
I don't care.

I don't like when people disrespect me.

I said let me find my own way home
and he followed me.

I make my own money
I have my own debit card
and I'm going to catch my own mother fucking subway home.

Period!

Like, why the fuck are you following me?

★

Isn't dating
horrible?

★

Send me a picture
of your dick. I'm sending
you a picture of mine right
now. Do you want me to
come? Talk to me. I'm in
a cab. Don't worry.
I'll give the driver a
big tip. Wait! He's pulling
over to let me out.
I'll call you back.

★

I should never ever
be in a bad
relationship
again
ever
ever
ever
as long
as I live
ever
it's better
to be
alone
it really
is
and if you want
a baby
get yourself
a baby
like
you don't
need
a man
no
you don't

So I emailed him this morning
saying basically
in sober mind mature as possible
I think this is reactive.
I was just trying to make one sober effort
to calm down from the fight
saying it's silly

a great month of trips together
adults don't break up
because they're both hung over
and snap at each other.
Cool off.
He's only had casual flings.
If he gets sick of someone
he just stops calling them.
He wrote back later in the day
he's conflicted
and I'd be crazy to settle
for less than I want.
I deserve more.
Which made me really sad
that he admitted that.
And it also frustrated me
because he's not an idiot.
Well, I don't know.
Everyone said Brady's partied in his twenties
at thirty he'll start worrying.
He grew up sheltered.
And spoiled.
One day he'll go through a wake-up call,
they say.
I think communication is a lost art.
I think he's a lost art.
I'm not sure but.
I wrote him a very long email tonight
I mean it was really long
saying
we don't need to figure out the long term
right now, I'm a grown woman
and can take care of myself,
and I like you,
I think you're a good person—
that kind of stuff.
I can appreciate your being 27.

I wasn't sure what he was going
to get back with.
He said I saw your message.
He was at his Yale secret society.
He's not supposed to tell anybody.
He said I'm not sure I can give you what you want.
Which is pretty mature, I guess.
People are mostly disappointing.

★

I need a fake boyfriend.
We don't need to like each other
but we need to pretend we do
for a half hour
or an hour.

★

Starting when I was a teenager
I had this shift of philosophy
I think you could call it
I would try to relate to a person
based on his understanding
of himself
how self-aware he was
not looking at his job or religion
or where he was from
or anything like that
and if he were on the edge
of society in some way
even if he had committed crimes
and he existed on the dark side

rather than the light
or just lived a very different life
than I did I wouldn't look
at his actions through the lens
of right and wrong
good or bad
but did he take responsibility
for his actions even atrocious ones
did he understand what motivated himself
what was pushing him forward
did he learn to control those forces
or did those forces control him?
That was what was
becoming interesting to me.

★

He's very cute. He's just a
Republican. You have to
  shape him. Tell him to speak.
    I mean that sounds
horrible
        but you've got to shape him
into who you want
    him to be.
You know what I mean?
Because when you first meet
someone
they're so
vulnerable
just like you are
just like he'll try
and shape you
into who he wants
you to be.

64

You know what
I mean?
        When you were in the
bathroom he wanted to know
        in detail about our time in
Florida. If he wouldn't
have said that. You have to
        remember. He gets wedding
invitations up the wazoo.

        I'm so I-don't-know.

You have to stop thinking that
way! He was very nice. To
        spend. To pay.

★

But Daddy you know
I've already sacrificed myself as a mother.
You know I rarely spend time with Cia.
Every time I leave the house
she cries I feel horrible
I'm working weekends
nights
and killing myself
all over the place
but they want me
there even more
and when I'm home to be reading
cardiology
which would be fine
if I were single
or married without child.
What do you think I should do?

In terms of my life my worry
is if I must leave this program
without a license
I will have no career.
I failed my boards a year ago.
Do you still think at age 30
I can take money
from my parents?
Sometimes I feel the goals
I set for myself
are not in line
practicing on people
paying out of pocket
bringing their kids from Saudi Arabia.
I don't feel I'm making a difference
in anyone's life

then today the director pulled me aside
said I didn't come prepared
I was a mess
I dropped a specimen on the floor.
I tried to explain
but damage was done.
People talk.
'This might not be
the program for everyone,' she said.
O my god.
Is she telling me to leave?
She said, 'No. I'm telling you
if you want to stay
you must give even more
than 100%—
more than 150%—
you must give completely!
Look, I'm a mother.
I worked part-time for years.
But this program makes it very difficult.'

She kept saying, 'There's no shame
in leaving.'

No one's reaching out a hand to me.
What should I do?
You saw me struggle through medical school
through residency.
Now this.
I can't shut the door on my child.
Say, 'Go away
do something else.'
My father said, 'Look!
You can do this.
Can you hear me?
We support you darling
no matter what.
Tell the director tomorrow
morning. You can be
the best fellow in this place.
You can!
I know you can!
You must tell her this!'

★

*I remember reading a book in Jill's
tiny kitchen 1977 downtown LA
as she was chopping vegetables
in the sunlight   in the window
I looked up
to her
and said
you know
you could tell
a lot about a person*

just by showing the way
he or she talked
a whole book could probably be written
without describing the speakers'
clothing or anything about them
just revealing
what they said
and how they said it.
True, Jill said,
you should try it.

★

Happy birthday, Bobber.
You pumped for dinner?
Dan's going to bartend naked?
Shut up.

★

Yo, Miguel, where you is?

★

Black don't crack!

★

AT&T be violatin' me!

★

LESBIAN PSYCHO DYKE—AND I'M PROUD OF IT!

★

What kind of girl is she?
She's very normal. (Yawn.)
She'll date a tall guy with blonde hair.
Next day date a short guy with black hair.
She goes on a ton of first dates.
Any kissing?

★

Connoisseurs get their steak medium-rare
if they really want to taste the meat
so the shit doesn't get burned, like.

★

Kiner's very flaky but Kiner is also in a lock.
He kind of goes with whatever is of interest to him
at that moment is probably the best way I could put it.
There are just people you know you can count on
and people you know you can't.
I'm not saying I wouldn't stay friends with them.
They're just not your go-to.
They're fun and that's fine in the moment.

The one thing I will say
which is the reason why my husband and I don't get
too angry at Kiner kind of angry but not angry-angry
is because he has absolutely no intention
to hurt anyone else.
My point is there's malice and there's not malice.

★

What the fuck is up with your shit, yo?

★

I thought the shabby chic decorating was very tastefully done.

I liked the four-bulb lighting fixtures especially the flush mounts.

I liked the floral burst chandeliers.

I did not love the tasseled material though

on the storage closets in the foyer.

I would've gone with mohair myself.

I loved the kitchen skylight

above the polished cerulean stone.

I liked their range

but they have an odd attraction

to yellow and green.

The fiberglass columns

were a problem—

I didn't want to say anything.

No, that's awkward.

It's very awkward.

I thought the kitchen was bigger, Jason, bigger in my mind.

It's huge—huge—compared to our kitchen.

I liked the white painted oak picture frames

of their kids when they were small

leading to the bathroom.

Did you think the master bedroom was huge?

No.

No?

The bed wasn't eleven feet from the screen, Janet.

It was only eight feet away

which was like sitting too close in a movie theater.

Our bedroom was much bigger.

★

Did you succeed in your mission to go anal?

★

...the state sucks.

★

Right after I've talked to them it's, like, 'Have I said too much?' and, like, 'I've had it.' I've barely said anything. It was annoying for me to check in with them because I couldn't really tell them anything that was going on. So I had to make up these other things that I didn't care about so I wouldn't care if they over-analyzed it because it didn't really happen. You know? So, yeah. There was this period of time when they were trying to schedule check-ins with me when I did not want to have check-ins with them. This is precisely what I mean when I say they were trying to solve a problem for me when it wasn't that big a deal. It wasn't something they could fix. I just felt like one of their projects, you know? They needed me for check-ins more than I needed them, and so that's why I left them behind.

★

You're being so vague and annoying.
Could you just tell me what's wrong?
Did you get a bill for the ambulance?

Everybody changes the ambulance bill!
Could you stop saying he'll be fine?
That's the worst thing you could say
and you've said it 700 times
this one conversation.

★

You know how easy it could be
for you not to feel this way?
You're bringing this on yourself.
You don't know how easy
it could be for you not to feel this way.
You're bringing this on yourself.
And I never really understood.
You're bringing this on yourself.

★

What did I do?
Oh shit fuck!
My father's going to kill me!
Drunk driving.
My license got suspended six months.
How will I get to work?
O, it feels so good to be outside.
Unfuckingbelievable.
To be down there.
Overnight.
In the Tombs.
Overpacked.
Bad news.
I slept one minute. How could I

sleep surrounded by lunatics?
I don't ever want to go back.
Cops robbed my wallet!
They have you packed in
with criminals. Guys who
jumped turnstiles
in the subway
have to wait
72 hours to see a judge.
Every hour they come by
to hand out these rubbery
cheese sandwiches.

★

No need to freak out
                    trying
to get pregnant
again.
Why are you stressing yourself
out?

★

She's very picky. She knows what
she wants. There's a word for
it. Reclusive. Her apartment
smells. Debby Downer.
        She has five cats.
Will she ever leave Huntington?

★

You look up
'quantitative easing'
and you'll find out
why the stock market
is doing so well.

★

It's funny.
She's into fashion.
But she always looks so crappy.

★

O my god all I remember
is they sold honey mustard pretzels!

★

I'm not going to etiquette school.
I'm from Paterson, New Jersey.

★

I like your big ass.
No, I do.

★

I see every object alive
and luminous
and at the same time I
see the decay and death
inherent in it's very shining.

★

Wait a minute—
you're talking vertical?

★

Hey!
He has a cyst off his spleen
that's malignant and
bright on the screen and
there's liquid seeping out and
if the liquid is blood
he could die
tonight!
To cut him open
would cost $6,000
and I don't have it. Oh, Barclay!
This is, like, the worst Monday
ever!

★

This guy's enraged. Obama
won he's fighting with his

wife I mean these guys
are nuts just apologize.
Hello? Hello? Hello? Hi.
Hello, Caroline? You want
to call me in the morning?
Call me anytime. Sorry
I woke you.
What's the spread?
Can you speak?
Are you home?
Just say yes or no.
Hamilton walked Sam.
I told them the meds I
take for hypertension.
They laughed.
They said half the people
in New York City have hyper-
tension. It's no big deal.
Girl, every inch every centimeter
counts.

★

It's your birthday.
You get special treatment.
Yeah, like.
You posted it and then
Henry posted it and now
everyone is just, like, focused on it
and it's, like, so annoying.

But, dude, actually
I'll be honest with you.
I'm definitely going
to come visit you

in Australia
because I want to go there
so badly and it's, like, an amazing
opportunity—
and, like—
you know it's funny—
this is going to sound cheesy—
our friendship will work out better
with you on the other side of the globe
than if you continued to live in
Queens.

★

She's so cool.
She's my ace boon coon.
Been to Harvard
but she's real real down.
She bought Don Kirshner's
house in New Jersey.
Remember when we used
to watch his rock concerts
on t.v.? He was such a
big drinker he had bars in bathrooms
and spas in places you'd never imagine.

★

'Make sure you get home,' he said.
What the fuck?
Like, why are you following me?
He kept following me.
Literally I walked three blocks

trying to get away from him.
You heard him on the phone, right?
You heard him on the phone.
Literally I walked three blocks.
And mind you all I had was one drink in the club
because I'm really not drunk.
I'm emotionally drunk because
I don't like when people disrespect me.
I can't fucking fight him.
You know what I mean?
It's different when a person on the street disrespects me
and I can fucking, like, line it up with you, like, you know?
He's a fucking pussy.
He's, like, 'I don't fight girls.'
You know I'll whoop your ass.
You know I'm from the streets, Timmy.
Timmy's never been in a fight his whole life.
One, two, three, you taught me
not to turn the fuck out.
He's, like, 'I'll just run.
If Chris come after me, I'll run.
If someone come after me, I'm just going to run.'
He'll keep running.
Like, you have asthma.
You can't run that mother fucking long.
I'm over it.
I don't like when people—
I'm going to hit you lower than you hit me.
Once you start me there is no fucking stopping.
You have to understand, like, I grew up on the streets.
Like, yeah.
He's so fucking privileged?
When I grew up
I grew up on the streets
and I don't like that disrespectful shit.
Period. I don't care if it's from a girl
or from whoever because I don't care

whether I lose or not
whether I lose or win
my cousins are still going to be
fucking waiting for you.
Period.
Period.
And I fucking own the shit.
He's, like, 'I want to make sure
you get home.'
We rode together, we lie together.
On Friday we went to a gay club
because I was supporting him
and I sleep with the gays, you know.
He saw a whole bunch of gay black guys
and he left me.
He left me!
Like, ooooo.
It was supposed to be no cover charge.
There was a $30 cover.
And he left me.
Now that we had this argument,
now that I'm on this phone with you,
he's, like, 'I just want to make sure you get home safe.'
Like, are you serious?
Like I don't know how to catch a subway? A taxi?
Like I don't have a debit card?
He's drunk right now.
He's such a protagonist.
I've known that about Tim
since I've been best friends with Tim
seven years.
He's, like, 'I don't protagonize, I'm a victimize.'
And I'm, like, what are you talking about?
After all that he said
he wants to make sure I get home safe.
That's bull.
He's, like, 'Chrystal knows me. Chrystal knows me.'

What does Chrystal know?
Chrystal knows shit about you.
Like, you think my bitch is going to choose you
over me? You're dreaming.
Get out of here.
You know something's got to make me pop off.
I don't just pop off randomly.
If I did I would be a shit every day.
Like, since you met me five seven years ago
whatever it's been you know I've only
popped off twice. Once with Boo
and once now.
I can't deal with drunken people
because they just say what they want to say.
He wants to say everything he wants to say.
I kept changing direction trying to walk away from him.
Multiple times. Multiple times.
I know he's my best friend
but I don't care who you are.
Clearly I don't care if you are my blood sister.
Once you cross that path, I will target you.
I don't care.
I'm, like, Tim, you have never been this way,
never talked to me this way, ever. I'm so confused.
I'm the one who's not drinking.
I'll have a shot with you guys just to cheer.
So for you to go, 'Oh, she's drunk.'
Like, what?
Tim, you've been with me when I was drunk
and blacked out.
For you to say this is drunk
it's because you're drunk.
You're wrong. You're wrong.
You pushed me to say these things.
You pushed me to hurt your feelings
because I wanted to speak the truth.
Because after I called you

after all the shit you was talking
you just want to make sure I'm safe?
What? I make more money than you.
I can get home fine.
I can get home perfectly fine.
But every outer way
every street way
he followed me.
We were going to fight on the subway.
I literally threw my shoes at him.
My fucking $600 shoes.
Because I don't fucking care.
He's, like, 'Why are you hitting me?'
But he knows what he does, babe.
I've seen him do it with so many people
since I've known him for seven years.
He switches up.
I've seen him do it.
But it's different when you do it to me.

★

It's kind of a really weird time in my life.
I'm trying to come to grips
with my lack of success
and what I should be doing
and where I should be going.
The career part was going
fairly well and now
that part just got taken away.
You know.
I don't know.

★

> Look at that
lobby—gorgeous! I never
> noticed it before.

What an interesting city.
Just look at the people!
Like, what are they all doing?

    ★

Elul, the new moon.
Soon they'll chop off
chickens' heads at daybreak.
I can't get into it.
Yet I yearn to be
close to G-d
every minute day in
day out
like I yearn
for art and poetry.
Art and Poetry
stay near—
please be my prayer
this new year.

    ★

Hey, dude!
The whole fucking game has changed.
There's a whole craft to it.
They make t.v. shows about it.
There's a t.v. show about a fucking chef.
There's a t.v. show about a fucking waiter.

Do you know what I mean?
So you can be, like, pseudo-famous.
You know what I mean?
To me I'm caught in the middle
of, like, you know
—I mean—
how old are you, bro?
       Me? I'm 60.
60?! You must be fucking Italian!
You look my age.
I easily look your age
and I'm 36.
You know what I mean?
You know, you got
more than enough swagger
from the front seat
of a fucking cab
through the mirror
through your head.
You got some fucking nice swagger.
You know what I mean?
And I'm not crawling up your arsehole, mate.
You know what I mean?
Do you know what I mean?
These days you can get famous
for fucking nothing.
Know what I mean?
They make a show about you for nothing.
Your mother will be terrified
of all the people that will fucking give you a show.
You know what I mean?
This is on you.
I'm looking at the back of your head
and the way you carry yourself.
Like, all I'm saying is you look good, mate.
And where I come from
that means a lot

because if you don't look good
you get a punch in the face.
You know what I mean?
There's no weapons.
No one's going to help you.
Someone's going to put you to sleep.
So me being from New Zealand
in a glance
and looking at you
and I do this often.
It's not like I fucking turned up
on the last doorstep.
Do you know what I mean?
I'm not saying it's a present either.
It's all you, bro.
Like, thank you.
And like I say
more often than not
old New Yorkers
do their shit
cool as fuck
and they understand.
Do you know what I'm saying?

Sorry.
Maybe I'm talking too much.
But fuck that.
If I crossed all the way
from New Zealand and talked,
I get to say a little bit o' my piece.
And I thank you.
And you look fucking great
at a glance
at a fucking glance.
Know what I mean?

PART 4

Vanessa's pregnant
and she doesn't know
whose it is.
She thinks it's a guy
she doesn't speak to anymore.
She's seeing a new guy
one month but one week
before he got on the scene
someone already put a seed
up there.
She says she really likes
the new guy.
I think he'll be cool
and understanding
when he finds out
and tries to work with
it.
He has two sons,
she has one daughter.
He may be cool.
I think he's cool.
I *hope* he's cool.

★

She left him at the altar
not once but twice.
She's, like, wild.
She's a man eater.
Men don't. She just has
men.
Her aloofness drives men
wild. I don't know about
now. But in her twenties
and thirties they'd fall all

over her. Her indecisiveness
drives men
wild.
She never married.
It's weird. She just went
through men. There's some
strangeness there.

I pass a drug test
then I think
maybe I should take drugs to celebrate.
Is that a normal thought process?
Probably not.

Dr. Collins calling.
I mean to say
with her anti-psychotic
medications is there anything at all
you could add?

Is there anything
you could give to quiet
her delusions?

Do you think it's weird of me
not to want to be a tax lawyer?

★

I've been studying molecular
parts of the brain.
I'm surprised you haven't
called me.

★

Shut the fuck up.
You shut the fuck up.

★

Listen, be good.
Listen, *you* be good.

★

Get the fuck out of my face.
You get the fuck out of *my* face.

★

You have to know one person really well
in this city where so many people are alone.

★

I wasn't alone. I was with 30,000 people.

★

Whaddya say?
     Who got a tooth out?
  What?

★

Got a fare from Astoria
to the Sutphin Boulevard train station.
My first time returning there
since high school 1972.
Same crowd
was hanging around
after midnight.
Flashy dressers.
The scene was marked
by a few sharks.
It looked different too.
The El was torn down.
Jamaica Avenue.
My father's mechanic
Russ Hawkins
lived on South Road
shot his wife in the crotch
went to jail.
Archer Avenue
where I went to yeshiva
was down the street.
A sewing factory occupied
the ground floor, and our

poor school rented the second floor.
How much I loved my friends back then,
our religion, our close way
of life, in school six days a week,
together on Saturday night,
together all summer somewhere
upstate. Always together. The way
we'd do anything to help each other.
And how fast I snapped
and felt I had to get
away from it all.
Some pressure inside me pushing, pushing.
I used to gaze through big windows
teacher was talking
and look at trains
pulling in and out
of Jamaica station
and wonder when
I would ride
away.

★

Like, if you can't put up the money,
like, if you don't have it
or you can't afford it
I'll find some other means
as in, like, let's try to move it forward.
So what are you waiting for?

I think he has the same problem
that too many other people have—
they can't stay in the energy
so they flip out
because I found a text he sent me

after the Dali Lama came
that got him flipped out about
where he was, like, 'Yeah, man,
it's awesome,
you're awesome,
blah-blah-blah!'
So I don't know
what bee got in his bonnet
but maybe this Pope thing
flipped him back around.

★

My second week behind the wheel,
2 a.m., two sleeping lovers in back,
temperature below zero,
I got lost in Williamsburg.
She muttered, 'Jeez, I think you could
invest in a GPS.' I left the cab
running at the curb
and asked directions in a bodega
where the clerk said,
'Why don't you just hop in a cab?'
I sighed, 'Because I am the cabdriver!'

★

I got in a cab a while back
what are the chances
getting a cabdriver
woman
white
English speaking

what are the chances?
I said okay.
Then I swear
three months later
I got in a cab
—it's the same driver!
What are the chances?
I understand the same driver
but white female?
Do you know who I'm talking about?

★

I got to dye my hair tonight.
What do you want to dye it?
Orange.
You should get your theme on.
She was crying one night and I
was, like, yo.
He was, like, walking by
and made eye contact. He was
at the lawn yesterday. A lot
of people got caught. A lot
of people at school think
he's gay because he's a new guy
and he's so small and effeminate.
I brought my birth control.
I don't get a heavy period
but if I do is that a problem?
Is the period shorter
on a contraception? Jake Bloom
is so hot. He, like, smashed me
against a wall
and started munching my neck!

*

I want someone to like my elbows.

*

It was slippery
seven seconds old.
I was afraid of dropping it.
Then
I realized
this
is my son.

*

Driver, do you mind if we have sex in the back seat?

No, I don't mind.

*

People say he like me
and shit.
Just cop from him, you say.
It's business.
I know that.

*

I feel so gross
getting married at the Waldorf.

★

John is the only really
religious person I know
I care what he thinks
about me.

★

You don't care about making money?
You don't care about making money?
What do you care about?

★

My mother could spot
a piece of lint
a hundred yards away.

★

He plays basketball at Vassar.
Like, what man goes to Vassar?

★

Stan, I want to talk to you.
When you're hailing a cab for us
you need to be stronger.
You need to be tough. Come on!
Don't let other people
take your cab.

★

Operator: 911. What's your emergency?

I'm a cab driver.
My cab broke down on the Manhattan bridge.
Have a police car back me up. Please!
No one can see me.
I'm standing outside the cab
waving away traffic
upper level going toward Manhattan.

You say you're a cabdriver, and what happened?

My cab is disabled! Can you hear me? It's on the side
going toward Manhattan. Hurry! Send a police car!
Can you hear me?

What bridge is that?

(louder) *THE MANHATTAN BRIDGE!*

What's your name?

Clifford Fyman.

What's your name?

CLIFF-ORD FY-MAN!

Sir, your yellow cab broke down,
Manhattan bridge, going toward Manhattan.
Is that correct?

Yes! Please hurry!

three minutes later...

Operator: 911. What's your emergency?

*It's me! The cabdriver
on the Manhattan bridge.
IT'S TOO LATE!
Someone smashed into the cab.
He smashed it really hard.
He was going really fast.
Send an ambulance!*

Is someone injured?

He must be. He hit it really hard!

Do you see he's injured?

No....

Take a look and see if he's injured.

*But everything's a mess! There's broken
glass everywhere! He almost knocked
the cab off the bridge!*

Do you see if someone's injured?

I'm, I'm going around the side to look...

HE'S GONE! HE'S COMPLETELY GONE!
HE'S GONE!

The driver left the scene?

YES HE'S GONE!

★

I rolled down the window
middle of night
told the guy in the Bronx
way up near Co-op City
his card
wasn't working
and I followed him
up the block.
He kept saying it was good
though he knew it wasn't.
'See the tip I left you?'
he said, which was worth nothing.
He walked right
into a darkened house. Click.
I didn't want to confront him.
He could've had a weapon.

★

I have a friend who entered law school at age 48.
People tried to talk him out of it.
They said when you get out of school you'll be 51.
He said I'll be 51 anyway.
I might as well be a lawyer.
Now he is a lawyer with a good job.

★

Daddy, when is my life going to get better?

★

*When she first spotted my cab I was starting to park on a
snowy side street at 2 a.m. to buy a cup of coffee and she
surprised me opening the door and said I could still buy that
coffee she'd wait but I said that's okay and we mapped a course
to Gowanus then skimmed across a conversation of the world's
religions and how her parents down south wanted her to
remain a Baptist but she wanted to explore Buddhism as the
snow fell and how a bad thing sometimes was a detour that
helped us escape something worse till we found our way which
was just like this detour she said through the side streets till we
came into the clear at Atlantic Avenue.*

★

wait the first night I didn't see you you blew me off.
the second night you helped me file a police report
and then you went off to the—
because I wouldn't go to the—whatever.
I didn't do anything.
I didn't do anything stupid.
O my god don't do that to me!
I don't have a guilty conscience I don't—
                              it's more
worried—
              I didn't do anything wrong.

101

*

You told me to go fuck myself.
Do you remember telling me
to go fuck myself?
Catherine, I know
you're my wife!
I have
my cab
coming to get you
now.
Catherine, I left you—
I left you—
I asked you—
I want you back—
CATHERINE!

*

Come to New York in January.
Like, freeze your balls off, man.
Thanks.

*

hey
I just wanted
to check in with you
talk to you
just let you
hey there's someone here
but at the same time

I really appreciated
our time together
I haven't told you yet
I want to tell you now
I'm kind of initiating it
hey

I mean he's a gypsy
I say I'm one
he's one
the definition of one
I see someone
who just wants to
hold me
this could be the one
who knows?
I may not have dated around
but I've slept around enough
to know
minimum dated
but I've definitely slept

★

I turned left at 39th and Park
a man hailed me
standing long blue overcoat
—Ron Padgett—
poet I've revered for years!
Soon as he said, 'Tenth Street and Second Avenue,'
I announced myself in the dark.
'Hi, Ron. This is Cliff Fyman!'
He cried out surprised as I was.
I reached my hand through the open

partition
shook his hand
declaring, 'This ride is free!'
Ron braked, 'Oh, no, it isn't!
You put that meter on right now
or I'm getting out of this damn cab!'
He went for the door.
I flipped the meter on.
I didn't want him running out.
He asked how I was doing.
Practically suicidal seconds ago
now I could say, 'GREAT!'
We chatted the whole way.
'Poet Dick Gallup—
he's my oldest friend,'
Ron said sadly
probably thinking of older friends now gone,
'drove cab 40 years
for the same San Francisco company.
Got promoted to dispatcher.'
'Tremendous!' I shouted,
adrenalin soaring.
'They had to know him well,' Ron figured,
'after working there 40 years.'
We touched on a variety of subjects:
Uber's cutting into 30%
of yellow cab business,
recent readings we'd been to.
I felt transported to a state
where all complaints fell away.
He recalled a painter he admired
who lived on my block
till she passed on, Jane Wilson,
exhibited at the Parrish Art Museum.
Friend to Jane Freilicher.
Her husband was art critic John Gruen.
Weaving the wide Sienna van

through a log-jammed intersection
I remarked, 'I don't want any accidents
with Ron Padgett in my cab.'
He returned my jest with his own beam—
'It would be in the NY Times.'

When I pulled up he asked me to sign
the receipt—seriously?—yes!
He'd sell it he said
to the Yale Library special collection
and get paid more for it
than the cost of the ride.
He shook my hand goodbye.
Wow!
What a ride!

SPEAK!
And use your words.
Use your words.
Speak!
Don't use violence!
Because violence overshadows
everything we're fighting for.
All of it.
Know this—we're living in a world of violence.
It's definitely not my forte.
It's not the world I want to live in.
I want to live in a world
where we're all happy
and we can be free.
And though I know this—
I know we're in a country
where the basis

the premise
is being free
but to me it's not
and to a lot of people it's not
and there needs to be more
into the light
we fighting to be free.
And we don't need violence
to show that.
We don't need violence.
To me we don't need violence
to show that.

But I get resistance.
It's like the constant
Malcolm X—Martin Luther King argument.
Like, what's the right way to go about
things?
Should we do violence
or should we push forward
in a non-violent way?
To me violence isn't the answer.
To me honesty is the answer.
I'm a lesbian.
I'm 23.
My mother is Puerto Rican.
My father came alone
from Cuba at age 14.
We need community.
Let's be honest
and fight this battle together.
And that's all we need.
And let us be honest
and fight this battle together.
And I will be there to fight
this battle together
with everyone!

AFTERWORD

The Genesis of My Taxi Cab Poems

In 2012 at age fifty-seven I went back to driving a yellow taxi cab at night in New York City. When I'd meet my friends Barbara Henning and Bill Kushner, I'd tell them the surprising things I'd heard passengers say into their cell phones and to each other in the back seat of the cab. It was often very raw stuff said as if I weren't there. I'd driven a cab in my twenties. Back then when a passenger got in, he or she would usually sit silently looking out the window or chat up the driver about the weather, local events, news of the day. Or they'd open an attache case and shuffle business papers.

That had changed. As soon as people got into the cab they'd flip on their phones.

Barb and Bill each said, "You've got to write this stuff down."

I'd written taxi cab poems in the 1970s and I didn't want to go over the same ground. But Barb and Bill prevailed upon me.

The first few weeks I had to concentrate totally on the driving aspects of my new job—the traffic signals, traffic patterns, how to get places, which lane to be in to make such and such a turn, how to work the meter. Things like that. After I got all that down pat, I focused on writing poems.

My ears were fresh to the new spoken material. Writing down what people said seemed far more interesting than describing the driving experience from my point of view. I started getting into it by writing in a small notepad at red lights and in traffic jams. Sometimes after the passengers exited, I'd catch up on what they said. I'd always enjoyed expressing creatively aspects of my job in poems and drawings while I was on the job. This taxi writing became the next step in the development of that interest. I liked making found poems from overheard speech ever since I read William Carlos Williams and tried it on the streets of Berkeley and then as a student at The Jack Kerouac School of Disembodied Poetics.

Barb offered to lend me her voice recorder. I turned down the offer. I thought I was doing OK writing quickly in a note pad. The narrative would get short-circuited by the light turning green and my needing to have both hands on the wheel. I liked the technique of the narrative suddenly snapping off then continuing someplace else.

Very late one night I drove a young African American teen to the edge of the FDR in an isolated section of Chinatown where he expressed a kind of rap or fast flow of words and syllables to his friend on the cell phone. His brilliant stream of words was keen as a Tracie Morris poem. Subculture language, syncopation, clipped consonants, speedy forceful rhythms. There was no way I could write that down fast enough! I sorely regretted not having Barb's recorder with me. I felt utterly discouraged I had missed a unique poem. The next day I went to B & H photo and purchased an inexpensive voice recorder which worked great. From then on, I used both my notepad and the recorder.

That night I learned my first important lesson. Even if I missed capturing a great poem which would happen now and then, don't get down, don't give up. Get ready for the next poem.

I started writing two or three poems a night. In the morning as soon as I woke up and washed my hands and face, I'd transcribe the poems into new files on my computer, and then I'd send the files to myself as email attachments. I'd have lunch and go. It was a long night shift. I'd leave home around 1:30 p.m. and ride my bicycle over the Fifty-ninth Street bridge to a fleet of 125 cabs in Long Island City where I would rent a cab at a garage located underneath the bridge. My shift went from 5 p.m. to 5 a.m. I would arrive at the grimy garage by 2:30 p.m. and wait on broken-down couches a couple of hours with other night shift drivers hoping to be dispatched a cab by 4:30 when some of the day shift drivers returned early. During those two hours of down time, I'd open my phone and read the poems I'd written the night before. I would make mental notes as to how I would shorten some of the lengthy first drafts. Basically, I became so involved with this project that I thought about it all the time. When customers asked me what I did besides driving a cab, I'd sometimes try out the poems on them. I'd drive all night and return the cab to the garage at 5 a.m. Then I'd ride my bicycle back over the bridge down 2nd Avenue to the East Village where I would make a bath and get ready to crash. But first I'd reread the poems I'd written so far. I found it a helpful barometer to read the poems at 6 a.m. when I was dog-tired. It gave me a sense of whether the poems had substance or not. If it had substance, I would remain interested and focused on it even though I was reading in a state of exhaustion. If the poem really wasn't any good, reading it at that hour made me awfully irritated.

When I woke up, I'd repeat the process: type new files of the previous night's poems and send them as usual to myself as an email attachment. Then I'd read them at the garage waiting to be dispatched the cab.

That's how things went for a couple of years. The meter rates had gone up sharply in late 2012, and Uber didn't exist yet, and so business was very good for a while. I averaged thirty customers a night. I drove four nights a week.

After two years I decided to give a reading and find out how the poems sounded to other poets and friends. Jeffrey Joe Nelson gave me a reading right away at Unnameable Books in Brooklyn.

The reading went well. Barb came and so did John Godfrey. My old roommate, Daniel Simon, the painter Raphael Eisenberg, my sister Sherry and my best friend from high school all attended. My photographer friend David Haas and cousin Shelley Fyman phoned their good wishes. Barb said the audience was into it especially all the young people. Barb and John each said this series of poems should include at least a couple of poems about myself—not just entirely the overheard conversations of others. I tried to shrug off their constructive criticism at first but eventually came to agree. I was glad I listened to them. Someone wanted me to come right over to a party at her house and read the same poems again. Someone else asked if he could publish them.

There was a lot of material left over after the reading that hadn't been touched on. In the past, after I'd read a certain kind of poem or published it, I'd move on to something else feeling the cat was out of the bag. Could I sustain a series of poems with consistent quality or had I shot my wad? To keep in the groove, I thought about Joe Brainard's *I Remember*. He was able to stay in that place of pleasure page after page. He showed it could be done. I also thought of *The Canterbury Tales* and how each person in the poem steps up to tell his story then steps back into line and gives the next person a chance to step up and speak. That's how I viewed the back seat of my cab. One person from a certain background would sit down in the seat, tell into the cell phone his or her story, then step out of the cab as the next passenger would get in and tell their story.

I reread *The Purgatory* by Dante. It gave me a sense of how deep, dark and complicated human emotions could be and how a poet shouldn't be afraid of expressing that. Along those lines Kerouac wrote, "Blow as deep as you want to blow."

Sometimes it was like observing dirty laundry. But there were parts worth saving. It could be the noisiest day of traffic, passengers having long, mundane conversations spoken in low tones, I could be overloaded with aspects of the traffic I needed to concentrate on, and yet if they said something worth saving, my ears picked up on it. There was something going on with my ears that had never happened before. My ears seemed to have developed a sixth sense. I was grateful and told myself to make the most of it while it lasted.

Over the next four years I gave three readings. Each reading later became one chapter in the manuscript making a total of four chapters. I didn't want to rush things. It was my bugaboo that I had never published a complete manuscript of poems in book form unlike some of my friends. I would join the party at poolside but never jump in. I wanted to get over my fears by completing this manuscript in a thorough way so that after it would be published, I would have no need to ever look back.

The influences of several poets I'd admired going far back in time kept welling to the surface of my feelings. I almost wished the collection would never be completed. It was wonderful to swim in the influence of so many beloved warriors. Bernadette Mayer's *Helens of Troy* appeared and recharged my battery, while her late 1970s depiction of idiosyncratic New Englanders in *The Golden Book of Words* stayed with me. The many alternatives to narrative poetry as exhibited around the Poetry Project were on my mind especially Anselm Berrigan's poems. I also had in mind Dael Orlandersmith's writing performances. I heard her read on New Year's Day at The Poetry Project many times. Her dramatic pieces were expressions of tough love of all the different ethnic types there were in New York City. I thought of Gary Snyder's "Two Immortals" from his book, *Turtle Island*. The day after I picked up Ron Padgett in my cab, I told Barb about it and she gave me the nudge I needed to write the poem I did. I'm just spelling out here where I think these poems came from.

The subject of rhythm and tempo kept my interest fresh. I listened for speech rhythms I hadn't yet made into poems. If the rhythm was new to me, I'd start writing it down no matter what the person was talking about. If they spoke loud and clear, I'd automatically start recording them, and if what they said wasn't interesting, I'd delete it at the end of the ride. I fished with a wide net. To sharpen my appreciation for rhythm, I listened closely to the music stations late at night especially in winter. There were frigid nights after one or two a.m. when you wouldn't see anyone walking on the street. They say it's a city that never sleeps but late at night in winter it sleeps. Believe me it sleeps. I'd find a music station I liked and turn it up loud. I listened on Tuesday nights to WKCR's "Honky Tonk" show, "Tuesday's Just as Bad" show of acoustic blues then electric blues, and soul singers on "Night Train" till 5 a.m. Every midnight David Dye's "World Cafe" from Philadelphia played progressive indy rock on WFUV. On Sunday afternoon WFUV played "Ceol na nGael: Music of the Irish" followed by a program about swamp rock with a d.j. who made clear the Cajun rock 'n' roll genre from the Bayou and its French Louisiana influences. WBGO jazz from Newark. Carol Miller classic rock on WQXR. I didn't try to find a music rhythm and write a poem that matched that rhythm.

I just wanted to pay extra notice and appreciate the rhythms heard in people's everyday speech patterns.

From the first reading it became clear to me that the order of the poems was significant. Which poem came next could alter the effect and meaning of what went before. The order created nuances, attitudes, implications—stuff like that. I worked hard on the order.

The poems would probably not have continued till 2017 as one long series had I not been willing to work on the order. And I probably would not have been of a mindset to spend so much time on the order had I not recently studied traditional portrait oil painting in the studio five years full-time. Colors are warm or cool. Warm colors come forward toward the viewer, cool colors recede from the viewer. Everyone probably knows that. But in making a realistic painting, getting it right to a certain degree is painstaking business. How do you make a warm color even warmer? You might think by adding more warm colors to it. But, no. You make it warmer by making the color next to it cooler. And vice-versa. You make a cool color even cooler by making the color next to it warmer.

That was the way my head worked as I ordered the poems. I'm not even sure how to explain it. It felt like my painting teacher Sharon Sprung was sitting on my right shoulder the whole time. It was probably something like if a poem needed to be lighter, I lightened its mood by placing a more serious poem next to it. When I changed intensity—"value" it's called in painting— in one area it shifted the intensity in other areas of the sequence. I kept balancing moods and emotions back and forth, back and forth, so that hopefully the poems would unfold in such a way that the pieces would bring out the best in each other.

I had complete faith in the process. It just took a ton of time to get it done.

—C. F.
7 May 2019

CLIFF FYMAN was born March 3, 1954 in St. Vincent's Hospital in Greenwich Village and grew up in Brooklyn, semi-rural eastern Long Island, and South Jamaica, Queens. Leaving school, he found his way to Berkeley in 1975 where he self-educated relying on the used bookstores on Telegraph Avenue. In the fall 1976 he attended the first S.F. Poetry Festival and heard Anne Waldman announce from the

stage the beginning of the Jack Kerouac School of Disembodied Poetics in Boulder. In March 1977, he rode a Greyhound bus through a blizzard in Wyoming to Colorado, and he studied at the Kerouac School that spring and summer. In 1979 he attended a workshop at The Poetry Project with Harris Schiff. His mimeographed chapbook *Stormy Heaven* was published by Misty Terrace press in 1981, and in 1982 he was awarded a fellowship from Creative Artists Public Service (CAPS) which included leading a year-long workshop at the Payne Whitney Psychiatric Clinic. He attended workshops in the early '90s at the PP with Bernadette Mayer. He worked on and off as a yellow taxi driver at night in New York City from 1974-84 and then again from 2012-2017. He has lived in the East Village since 1979 giving many readings and publishing in magazines and anthologies. This is his first full-length book.

Photo at Cafe Pick Me Up by Barbara Henning

Acknowledgments

I want to acknowledge and thank Barbara Henning, David Haas, Peter Bushyeager, my late cousin Shelley Fyman and Ted Cohen for reading the manuscript and making valuable suggestions. A special thanks to David Haas for his assistance with the cover image.

I also want to acknowledge the editors who published some of the poems in these magazines: Stephen Baraban, *Bandoneon*; Dave Roskos, *Big Hammer*; David Cope, *Big Scream*; Al Markowitz, Mary Franke, *Blue Collar Review*; David A. Kirschenbaum, *Boog Reader*; Jamey Jones, *Hurricane Review*; Jeffrey Cyphers Wright, *Live Mag!*; Martin Cohen and Thomas Scarborough who accompanied my poem with an original illustration by Tessa den Uyl, *Philosophical Investigations*; Amanda Deutch, Susan Brennan, *Saturday I Spent at Coney Island*; and Bernard Meisler, *Sensitive Skin*.

And finally, thanks to the curators who invited me to read my taxi poems for their series—Greetings Readings at Unnameable Books, WKCR FM "Art Waves," Torn Page, Zinc Bar, Dixon Place, LaMaMa, Social Justice Center of Albany, and Parachute Literary Arts. Poems from *Taxi Night* can be heard online at WKCR FM "Art Waves" archive, Poetry Thin Air, Penn Sound, and at DonYorty.com.

Long News Books
longnewsbooks@icloud.com

CPSIA information can be obtained
at www.ICGtesting.com
Printed in the USA
BVHW031937030222
628002BV00003B/177

9 780964 559141